D0077980

Student Obesity:
What Can the Schools Do?

by
Phillip M. Wishon

Library of Congress Catalog Card Number 90-60211
ISBN 0-87367-305-0
Copyright © 1990 by the Phi Delta Kappa Educational Foundation
Bloomington, Indiana

This fastback is sponsored by the Carnation Northeast Ohio Chapter of Phi Delta Kappa, which made a generous contribution toward publication costs.

Table of Contents

Introduction

In recent years the problem of child and adolescent obesity in the United States has been the subject of a National Institute of Health workshop, congressional hearings, and wide media attention. Obesity is a health hazard as urgent as any life-threatening disease. Expatriate Russian novelist Vassily Aksyonov makes the comment: "Nowhere else [except in America] have I seen so many overweight young people" (*In Search of Melancholy Baby*, Vintage Press, 1989).

In the United States, obesity has been called our primary health defect. Its relationship to diabetes and cardiovascular disease is now acknowledged. There is growing concern about childhood obesity and its possible association with later obesity. Although it cannot be said with certainty that childhood obesity results in adult obesity, children who are obese at seven years seldom change their body build and constitution at later ages. We do know that many factors contribute to child and adolescent obesity. However, treatment of this serious problem has been woefully inadequate.

Obesity is singularly detrimental to physical fitness as measured by muscle strength, cardio-respiratory endurance, flexibility, and body composition (degree of fatness). Studies show that youth fitness has not improved in the last 10 years, and in some cases has declined. The latest study conducted in 1985 by the President's Council on Physical Fitness shows that 40% of boys ages 6 to 12 cannot do one pull-up. When compared with a similar study in 1975, there has been no improvement in physical fitness. Similar bleak findings were reported by the national Children and Youth Fitness Study conducted by the U.S. Department of Health and Human Services in 1985. When children's body composition values were compared with a group of children tested in the 1960s, the study concluded that, on the average, children are fatter now.

In this fastback I shall examine issues attendant to child and adolescent obesity, review causes and consequences of obesity and related eating disorders, and offer some suggestions for the school's role in prevention and treatment of this pervasive health problem.

Definition and Assessment of Obesity

Obesity is defined by the National Dairy Council as a condition wherein there is an excess of body fat when compared with some standard or range of acceptable degrees of fat tissue for a particular population. Similarly, the Committee on Nutrition of the Mother and Preschool Child has defined obesity as a clinical presentation characterized by "excessive fatness." There is no consensus, however, as to what constitutes excessive fatness or how it is to be measured. Most nutritionists and pediatricians agree that an individual above the 85th percentile of weight in relation to height on the growth charts should be considered obese and may be at risk for developing adult obesity. Individuals have been classified as overweight if their relative weight/height for age is 10% greater than the expected standard as indicated by the growth charts.

With respect to routine monitoring of body weight, a note of caution is in order. While individuals more than 20% above ideal body weight may be defined as obese, any adolescent whose weight is more than 10% *below* ideal body weight should be evaluated further with a detailed dietary intake record and review of recent weights. An ongoing pattern of weight loss may be due to intentional dieting, anorexia nervosa, depression, or chronic illness.

Currently, the most objective and best correlated indirect measure of body fatness is the thickness of the skinfolds at specific locations (triceps and beneath the shoulder blades) as measured with skinfold calipers. The measure of skinfold thickness enables the clinician to arrive at a good approximation of how fat a child really is. These measures have been well correlated with body density and hence with the fat content of the body. They are particularly useful during childhood when lean body weight is constantly rising due to growth of the child.

It is widely agreed that a triceps skinfold in excess of the 85th percentile for children or adolescents of the same age and sex would be an indication of obesity. Obviously, this indication represents a statistical rather than a pathological definition. Age- and sex-specific percentile standards for both triceps skinfold thickness and upper arm circumference have been established and may be useful to clinicians in evaluating children and adolescents with either nutritional excess or deficiency.

Prevalence of Obesity Among Youth

According to a Harris Poll conducted for *Prevention Magazine* (November 1988), nearly two-thirds of Americans age 25 and over are too fat, and more than a third are at least 10% over the recommended weights for their height, body build, and sex. It is estimated that 20% of Americans are enough overweight to be at risk for certain diet-related diseases. The President's Council on Physical Fitness has concluded that 40% of children ages 5 to 8 years show at least one heart disease risk factor, such as obesity, elevated cholesterol, or high blood pressure.

It is estimated that obesity in adolescents has increased 39% over the past 10 to 15 years, with estimates ranging from 5% to 22% of adolescents being obese. An additional 5% to 10% of adolescents are overweight in that they are 10% to 20% above ideal weight. For every 100 children, it is estimated that at least 16 are obese.

In some population subgroups, such as children from low-income families or children with obese parents and siblings, the rates of obesity are considerably higher. By late adolescence, factors correlated with obesity include being female, black, of lower socioeconomic status, and having at least one obese parent. Approximately 80% of obese adolescents go on to become obese adults, and they tend to be more obese than those whose obesity developed during their adult years.

Relationship of Obesity to Other Health Problems

Excess weight puts undue strain on the human body. Obese individuals are more likely to suffer from cardiovascular disease, diabetes, gall bladder problems, osteoarthritis, respiratory problems, and varicose veins. Obesity is often present in association with certain kinds of cancer, elevated cholesterol, and glucose intolerance. The obese also are greater surgical risks and have a notably shorter life expectancy. Our bodies are simply not made to lug around an abundance of excess fat.

Obesity is among the most important risk factors associated with cardiovascular disease – currently accounting for nearly one-third of all deaths in the United States. Factors that predispose individuals to cardiovascular disease are thought to develop during early childhood. Indeed, the disease is believed to develop slowly as a result of the presence of excess fat or lipids in the blood, hypertension, obesity, and lack of physical activity. Obese adolescents have an alarmingly high incidence of multiple coronary heart disease risk.

It is well established that sustained hypertension in adults contributes to the development of coronary artery disease, congestive heart failure, cerebral vascular disease, and renal insufficiency. The prevalence of hypertension is nearly three times higher among the overweight, and it has been indicated that about two-thirds of mildly hypertensive adolescents will become hypertensive adults.

In addition to the medical problems associated with obesity are the psychological consequences. Social stigmatization directed at obese children is well documented. These youngsters are frequently ridiculed and often avoided. Rejection by peers often leads to withdrawal, isolation, and a diminished self-esteem. The obese adolescent's response in many cases is overeating and retreating into sedentary activities, thus exacerbating the problem.

Causes of Obesity

We now know that environmental, psychological, and genetic factors all play a role in the etiology of obesity, although it is difficult to isolate them. The level of food intake and physical activity are environmental factors contributing to obesity. But genetically determined metabolic factors control the number and size of fat cells in an individual. When psychological factors are added, the etiology of obesity becomes even more complex.

The average daily caloric needs of adolescents are 2,200 for girls and 2,800 for boys. These will vary, of course, depending on size and activity level of the individual. Contrary to popular belief, obese adolescents do not necessarily consume more calories than their normal-weight peers. However, they do differ in their eating behaviors in that they are more likely to skip meals and to eat less frequently. In addition, the obese adolescent is significantly less physically active and therefore less physically fit.

Television viewing is one passive sedentary activity that has been causally linked to childhood obesity. Research by W.H. Dietz of the New England Medical Center in Boston has shown that time spent viewing television is directly related to the prevalence of obesity in both children and adolescents. Furthermore, time spent viewing television in children ages 6 to 11 proved the most powerful predictor of the development of obesity during adolescence. Moreover, children watching television are prone to between-meal snacking — often eating the high caloric foods they see advertised on the TV screen.

Treatment for Obesity

Diet and exercise have been the standard medical recommendations for treatment of obesity. However, each year brings at least one new "proven" diet book that preys on the gullible. Some years back there were starvation or the zero calorie diets, which soon waned in popularity because of such problems as hypotension, kidney stones, and loss of protein. These were followed by the introduction of diets with only small amounts of protein. Gradually, these evolved into very low calorie diets. A major problem with all of these diet books is that people follow them without medical supervision.

Intervention with Obese Young Children

The best intervention strategies for treating obesity in young children is the establishment of healthful eating habits. This responsibility falls primarily to parents, but teachers can provide reinforcement in the classroom. Eating on the run, snacking excessively, and skipping regular meals are just a few of the activities that tend to interfere with good eating habits. Parents should provide young children with three nutritious meals daily, preferably at about the same time every day. They should be offered a variety of acceptable foods, with small to modest servings. While not denying a child a favorite non-nutritious food item, they should be restricted for special occasions. Also, using such foods as bribes can reinforce overeating. Praise, smiles, and hugs are much more effective means of reinforcement, both physically and emotionally.

A nutritious diet includes items from the four basic food groups (see Table 1). Mealtimes provide an opportunity for children to learn about nutrition as they partake of foods from these four groups.

Table 1. Recommendations for children's diet.

Meat group: Two servings daily from this group are recommended. Lean meats, fish, poultry, eggs, and cheese are all good sources of protein, fat, and vitamins.

Milk group: Children should have about one quart of milk daily. Other dairy products, such as cheese and ice cream, may also be considered as milk products. These foods are good sources of protein, fat, calcium, phosphorus, and vitamins.

Vegetable and fruit group: Four servings daily from this group will provide vitamins and, to a lesser extent, carbohydrates and minerals. At least one of the recommended four servings should be a food high in vitamin C, such as oranges or fruit juices fortified with vitamin C.

Bread and cereal group: Four servings daily from this group are the primary source of carbohydrates. Foods from this group also provide some protein, vitamins, and minerals.

The way children eat can be as important as what they eat. Avoid engaging in television watching while eating. Avoid bringing up serious family problems. Keep mealtimes relaxed, focusing conversation on the day's activities. In such a setting good eating habits are established, which will persist throughout life.

Snacks in the Diet

Many young children seem to need some food between meals. If properly selected, snacks can contribute to a good overall nutrition program. Snacks should be selected from the four basic food groups. Hard-boiled eggs, raw vegetables, fruits, and cheeses are excellent snacks and contribute to the well-balanced diet that children need. A glass of water or fruit juice will satisfy thirst (which young children sometimes mistake for hunger). To be avoided are snack foods that add only empty calories.

Snacks should be served at least an hour and a half before meals so as not to diminish a child's appetite at mealtimes. They should be offered at the same times each day, and children should refrain from engaging in any other activities while they are eating. Aside from planned nutritious snacks, children's contact with food between meals should be minimized. If children are absorbed in other activities throughout the day, they will give little thought to food.

Exercise and Young Childen

Many overweight young children do not eat any more than normal-weight children; their obesity results from their lack of physical activity. Lack of physical activity contributes to obesity as much as does excessive food intake. Most young children are naturally active; those under the age of six who are inactive may be in need of medical attention.

The lack of regular physical activity contributes to obesity in two ways: 1) without sufficient exercise unused calories are incorporated into fat storage deposits, and 2) the normal internal mechanism regulating appetite and satiety does not operate properly at low levels of physical exercise. To help maintain a positive energy balance, children should engage in any moderate physical activity they enjoy every day.

Markedly inactive obese children may need a planned regimen of physical activity. They should be started slowly following the recommendations of a health specialist. If skipping is too vigorous, they might begin by taking brisk walks. Other good ways for children to burn calories include jumping rope, jogging, swimming, riding a bicycle, hiking, and playing active games. A good level of energy expenditure requires 15 to 20 minutes per session. Aerobic activities involving the larger muscles in wide sweeping movements are especially good.

Physical activities involving a high degree of skill are not appropriate for the child who is poorly coordinated. But many physical activities can be linked to things a child enjoys doing, such as dancing to music, riding a tricycle, rollerskating, or kicking a ball. Parents or other adults can help children become more physically active by taking them to parks, playgrounds, and swimming pools and by participating with them in a variety of physical pursuits.

Weight loss should not be the goal in treating obesity in young children. Rather, by controlling food intake at the lower limits of normal requirements as determined through medical consultation and by increasing physical activity, the young child will "grow into" the stabilized body weight. The goal is to create a new energy balance based on nutrient intake at the lower limits of normal requirements and increased exercise.

Intervention with Obese Adolescents

Treating adolescent obesity is much more complex. Adolescents are less responsive to adult supervision and direction. They frequently enter into weight reduction programs without medical supervision. And they are extremely vulnerable to fad diets that promise immediate weight loss but can be damaging to their health.

In the past several years, health professionals have developed comprehensive weight management programs that seem to be effective over the short and long term. Laurel Mellin, director of the Center for Adolescent Obesity, University of California School of Medicine in San Francisco, has identified a list of characteristics of comprehensive low-risk intervention weight management programs. Such programs include the following:

Comprehensive assessment. Because of the multiple causes of obesity, the adolescent needs to have a comprehensive assessment prior to treatment. The assessment attempts to identify biological, behavioral, psychological, and family factors that might be contributing to obesity. Then intervention strategies are tailored to meet the needs of the adolescent and the family.

Nutritionally protective. During this period of rapid physical development, there should not be drastic reductions of food intake. It is better to allow small portions of food they enjoy (pizza, spaghetti) rather than to prohibit them completely. It is important that obese youngsters do not feel "different" when they are with their peers. Nutrition recommendations should be consistent with Recommended Dietary Allowances for a preventive diet for this age level. Average weight loss should not exceed one to two pounds per week.

Physical activity. Regular exercise is a core component of the adolescent's weight reduction program. The exercise program includes activities that improve endurance, flexibility, and strength. Emphasis is on those activities that are likely to be continued in adulthood.

Extensive family intervention. Critical to the success of adolescent weight reduction programs is extensive parental involvement. Separate sessions for parents conducted by a mental health professional focus on the family's role in modifying diets, scheduling exercise, and positive parent-child interaction.

Psychologically beneficial. Intervention strategies are designed to enhance self-esteem and improve body image. Techniques that might be psychologically stressful, such as aversion therapy and rigid or restrictive diets, are avoided.

Coordinated health care. The weight reduction program is coordinated by a group of health professionals. A physician assesses the adolescent's health prior to any interventions and monitors health status during treatment. Other professionals are available to the adolescent and family, including a mental health worker, registered dietitian, and licensed exercise physiologist.

Long-term, follow-up care. The maintenance of lifestyle changes in diet and exercise often requires continued support for an extended period. Supportive counseling should be available to the adolescent and family for at least one year after the intervention.

Studies of intervention efforts with obese adolescents confirm that a moderate program of diet and exercise reduces the risk of coronary heart disease and reduces blood pressure and serum cholesterol levels. Also, intervention programs that incorporate behavior modification techniques result in both short- and long-term improvement. Threats or scare tactics are not effective with adolescents and will often lead to cessation of treatment.

Because of ignorance or out of desperation to lose weight, adolescents are easy targets for diet fads. And there is no shortage of con artists to exploit them. Their products range from the ludicrous (spoons with holes in them) to the outright dangerous (diets based on consuming only one food product or the use of appetite suppressants that make outlandish claims for rapid weight loss).

With adolescents, it must be stressed in the strongest terms that there simply are no quick fixes for losing weight. If the method is too quick or too easy, it is probably a short-term fix at best and dangerous at worst. We need to make adolescents understand that an effective weight management program requires a balanced diet, regular exercise, persistence, and a lot of patience. Further, obese adolescents should be advised to seek nutritional and medical counseling before contemplating a weight reduction program.

Weight Management with Special Populations

The schools serve several special populations that present a variety of weight management problems. These include pregnant teenagers, the physically and mentally handicapped, and victims (mostly females) of eating disorders such as anorexia nervosa and bulimia.

Weight Management for Pregnant Teenagers

More than a million teenagers become pregnant every year, resulting in close to a half million live births. In addition to being a major social problem, pregnancy poses serious health problems for the young women themselves and for their babies. Adolescent females in general are at risk nutritionally, but a pregnant teenager is at even greater nutritional risk.

Several studies have found pregnant adolescents to have poor dietary habits. According to Dr. Mary Story of the Adolescent Health Program at the University of Minnesota Hospital and Clinic, pregnant teenagers' high consumption of low nutrient snacks and their erratic eating habits may preclude intake of recommended nutrients. Meal skipping, notably breakfast, may increase the risk of ketosis, which has been associated with higher rates of perinatal mortality. Since pregnant teenagers are disproportionately from economically disadvantaged populations, they may lack adequate food resources.

A combination of low prepregnancy weight and low weight gain during pregnancy is directly associated with low birth weight of the newborn. Nutritional deprivation during the first three months of pregnancy is associated with congenital defects in the fetus. Another critical period of nutrient influence on fetal development is during the last 15 weeks of gestation. Although optimal weight gain for pregnant adolescents is not known, it appears to be greater than for mature women, according to Dr. Story.

Inadequate weight gain may occur in pregnant adolescents if they are attempting to conceal their pregnancy or are involved in substance abuse. The possibility of an eating disorder also should be considered. Excessive weight gain is a problem in some teenage pregnancies. Although severe dietary restriction to limit weight gain during pregnancy is seldom, if ever, advisable, a weight reduction program may be necessary after delivery.

Physically and Mentally Handicapped Students

Obesity only compounds the daily adjustment problems faced by physically and mentally handicapped students. It is one more thing that sets them off from their nonhandicapped peers. Any weight management program for these students will require active parent participation. By working closely with parents of special needs children and monitoring their diets while in school, teachers can instill sound nutrition practices that will serve them throughout their lives.

Because handicapped students frequently have poor coordination, there is a tendency to excuse, or exclude, them from the regular physical education programs. Without regular exercise opportunities, these students fall into a pattern of sedentary activities, which only exacerbates their weight problems.

The American Alliance for Health, Physical Education, Recreation, and Dance and the Joseph P. Kennedy, Jr. Foundation provide suggestions about facilities, playground equipment, active games, and fitness activities that are appropriate for special needs students. Also, parents need guidance as to exercise options that are within the physical capabilities of their handicapped children. When handicapped children are involved in appropriate exercise activities, it not only serves as a weight management strategy but also enhances their physical coordination, cardiopulmonary fitness, and self-esteem.

Victims of Eating Disorders: Anorexia Nervosa and Bulimia

No longer considered rare, anorexia nervosa and bulimia pose a major health problem among young women in the United States. Some of the medical complications of these eating disorders are life-threatening. The onset of these eating disorders often occurs in early adolescence. Therefore, it is important to identify those at risk as early as possible so they can receive treatment.

These eating disorders reflect an obsession with thinness, even among adolescent girls who are of normal weight. In a 1986 survey of 271 adolescents of both sexes, researchers at Children's Hospital of Eastern Ontario found that almost half the girls *thought* they were too fat, when in fact 83% were normal weight for their height. By contrast, boys who thought they were too fat tended to be obese. Of the girls surveyed, 15% had induced vomiting to lose weight, whereas less than one percent of boys had done so (Feldman et al. 1986). A recent U.S. Public Health Service survey on adolescent health reveals that 51% percent of teenage dieters said they fast to control weight, 16% reported use of diet pills, and 12% admitted they vomit after eating. These statistics are almost certainly conservative since many victims of eating disorders are secretive and unwilling to acknowledge their problem.

Anorexia nervosa is a complex psychosomatic disorder, with 90% to 95% of its victims being adolescent females or young women. They tend to be bright, verbal, and assertive with a strong need to control their environment. According to the American Psychiatric Association, anorexics are obsessed with the fear of becoming obese and have a distorted body image. Anorexic behavior is characterized by avoidance of food, compulsive dieting, and excessive physical activity.

In their relentless pursuit of thinness, anorexics lose control over their bodies, disrupting the brain area that controls appetite, destroying the balance of other body systems, and ultimately starving themselves to death. As many as 75% of anorexics have been hospitalized at least once during the period of treatment. Physiologic problems associated with anorexia include essential organ derangement resulting from malnutrition, irregular heartbeat, hypertension, and ECG abnormalities. Pubertal delay is often evident among anorexics, especially amenorrhea (absence of menstruation).

Treatment for anorexia involves continued medical management combined with psychotherapy. The school's role in treatment is to identify early anorexia behaviors and refer the victims and their families to appropriate medical and psychological resources.

The word bulimia is derived from the Greek words for "ox" and "hunger." This eating disorder was so named because the victim eats like a hungry ox, that is, the bulimic indulges in eating binges. The gorging process, usually done secretively, can go on for hours and leaves the victim feeling bloated. The binge is followed by episodes of purging accomplished by vomiting or use of laxatives, diuretics, enemas, compulsive exercising, and weight-reducing drugs (amphetamines). Eventually, a compulsive pattern develops of eating binges, purging, and then periods of fasting.

A variety of health problems result from prolonged bulimia. Frequent and repeated vomiting can lead to erosion of the enamel of the teeth, inflamed esophagus, cardia arrhythmia, EEG abnormalities, and sore throat. Laxative and diuretic abuse contributes to damage to the colon, urinary infection, impairment of kidney functions, and chronic indigestion.

The onset of bulimia typically occurs in late adolescence and is predominantly a middle- or upper-class white female disorder. A conservative estimate is that at least 5% of adolescent females show occasional bulimic eating patterns. Often the eating binge is in response to an intense emotional experience, such as stress, loneliness, depression, or anger. Personality characteristics associated with bulimia include perfectionism, unreasonable goals and expectations, and low self-esteem. Like anorexia nervosa, bulimia is an addictive and self-destructive method of weight control. Psychotherapy and other forms of therapy usually are necessary to treat this eating disorder.

The School's Response to Student Obesity

The school's response to student obesity can take many forms. Foremost among these is establishing a climate of wellness throughout the school environment. The total school atmosphere should be a model of healthy lifestyles. Educational programs and counseling services should be available for obese students and their families. This chapter describes some of the things schools can do to help the obese student.

Promoting Sound Nutritional Practices

Students today are bombarded with books and other information about diets and dieting. Say "diet" and most people think of weight loss. But these days, a glance at the nutrition section of any bookstore reveals titles that go far beyond the shedding of pounds and slimming of thighs. "Follow our diet," claim the authors, "and you can stay out of the cardiac-care unit, avoid cancer, eliminate pain, boost your immune system, stay young, live longer — even think better." It can be tough to resist these diets that promise everything but an afterlife. But the lessons the schools must teach with regard to diets is simple: Don't believe in miracles. The dietary counsel students receive at school should be applicable for the rest of their lives.

While all students need a solid foundation in basic nutrition concepts, obese students require special attention. To help them with weight reduction, educators need to affirm them as persons and support them in their efforts. In particular, obese students must be discouraged from crash dieting. In addition to being dangerous to health, crash dieting usually results in temporary weight loss that is soon regained, leaving the student frustrated, depressed, and fat.

The lives of students today are full of activities in and out of school where eating takes place, usually in the form of snacks. While it is impractical to avoid snacks completely, obese students can be guided in monitoring their snack intake, including beverages. When food is served at school functions, the school can set an example by always including some low-calorie but nutritious snacks. The school also can make students aware of the high calorie snacks and suggest alternatives.

Fast-food restaurants are very much a part of teenage culture today. They do more than $20 billion worth of business a year, with teenagers being their major customers. Fast-food items typically are low in fiber and vitamin A and C, high in fat and sodium, and loaded with calories. It would be futile to try to keep young people away from fast-food restaurants. A more positive approach is to help them make nutritionally sound decisions about what to order. Table 2 shows comparisons of the caloric and fat content of standard fast-food fare. Using a chart such as this in the classroom can help students become aware of alternatives in fast-food restaurants for those who need to reduce their fat and calorie intake.

Promoting Physical Fitness

Regular physical activity and exercise is beneficial to good health. Studies have shown that regular physical activity is associated with fewer coronary risk factors (obesity and hypertension) and has a favorable effect on serum cholesterol and lipoprotein levels. There is evidence linking increased physical activity with a reduction in osteoporosis, in the incidence of Type II diabetes mellitus, and in the symptoms of anxiety and moderate depression. Moreover, studies in

Table 2. Comparisons of caloric and fat content in sample meals at fast-food restaurants.

High Fat Meals

Menu	Calories	Grams Fat
1. Double Burger with Sauce Milkshake French Fries (reg.)	1,275	65
2. Chicken Nuggets (6) Apple Pie Coffee with Cream	655	40
3. Fish Sandwich with Cheese & Tartar Sauce Soda (12 oz.) French Fries	855	40

Low-Fat Alternative Meals

Menu	Calories	Grams Fat
1. Beef Tacos (2) Low-Fat Milk (8 oz.)	495	22
2. Single Burger Tossed Salad (Low-Calorie Dressing) Low-Fat Milk	445	16
3. Baked Potato (Plain) Margarine (1 Pat) Tossed Salad (Low-Calorie Dressing) Low-Fat Milk	340	7
4. Cheese Pizza (1 Slice) Tossed Salad (Low-Calorie Dressing) Orange Juice (8 oz.)	315	6

(Source: Massachusetts Medical Society)

both children and adults have shown that increased levels of regular physical activity are associated with improved scores on tests of physical fitness.

Students who are physically fit look better, feel better, and feel better about themselves. This is a message that must get through to obese students. When schools help students to become physically fit, they are laying a foundation for lifelong wellness. In a school where fitness is emphasized for all, it creates an environment conducive to a variety of exercise programs that can be tailored for the obese student.

Communicating with Parents

Parents must be involved in whatever the schools attempt to do to help the obese student. Regular communications to parents about sound nutrition, dangerous crash diets, physical fitness, and eating disorders will help them to reinforce in the home what the school is trying to do. If the school offers an organized weight reduction program, parents should be encouraged to enroll their obese child in it. Parents should be invited to participate in a school-sponsored physical fitness program, thus encouraging exercise as an integral part of the family's lifestyle.

Following are 19 suggestions for assisting students and their families in dealing with the problem of obesity:

1. Support parents' efforts to provide good nutrition in the home by providing them with a variety of print and nonprint educational materials on nutrition.
2. Encourage parents and children to plan and prepare nutritious snacks to eat between meals.
3. Encourage older children to plan and prepare family meals that reflect nutritional balance.
4. Provide parents with information on how to check packaging labels to determine nutritional adequacy.

5. Organize health fairs to provide students with information on nutrition, physical fitness, and lifelong health behaviors. Involve community health care agencies.
6. Sponsor workshops on topics relevant to students' interests:
   a. preparing quick but nutritious breakfasts.
   b. preparing nutritious snacks.
   c. exercise programs that fit student lifestyles.
   d. avoiding excessive television viewing.
7. Encourage local parks and recreation departments to sponsor physical fitness and weight control programs for youth.
8. Help students design an individual wellness plan, which they can implement right away.
9. Enlist older students to design and implement a nutrition and exercise program for younger students and their parents.
10. Design and teach a lesson on selecting a balanced nutritional meal from a fast-food menu.
11. Start a campaign to eliminate empty calorie items from school vending machines and replace them with nutritious items.
12. Develop fitness programs in schools using noncompetitive, low-skill games and activities that are fun.
13. Promote walkathons, aerobics classes, and "stretchercize" programs among students and teachers to create a community of fitness advocates.
14. Use "teachable moments" to focus students' attention on such issues as fad diets, malnutrition, cardiovascular fitness, being "skinny" versus being healthy, etc.
15. Inform students about eating disorders (anorexia, bulimia, sugar junkies) and their implications for health.
16. Have students create posters on nutrition and fitness to display at shopping malls and radio spots and TV news briefs to be broadcast on local radio or television stations.
17. Enlist student volunteers to work with community agencies on fitness and wellness campaigns.

18. Conduct staff development workshops on wellness issues and on ways of identifying students with nutrition and related health problems.
19. Institute nutrition and fitness counseling for students identified as at risk.

Bibliotherapy for the Obese Student

In addition to counseling, reading books can help students come to terms with the emotional stresses of obesity. Fortunately, there is a good selection of children's and young adult fiction in which the central character has a weight problem. A list of these books and recommended grade levels is included in the Appendix. Through reading these books, students can see how persons their own age have coped with the problem of obesity. Such reading is a form of bibliotherapy in that students identify with the characters and situations and develop insights into their own problems with obesity.

Conclusion

The consequences of obesity for the physical health of students are life threatening, and the emotional consequences are debilitating. The schools, in cooperation with parents and community health services, can play an important role in the identification and treatment of student obesity through screening programs, education, and counseling. The future health of our youth depends to a great extent on their receiving accurate information. Education and counseling on the maintenance of proper weight and a regular exercise program should be provided in all schools.

Educators should make schools places where healthy lifestyles are practiced. They should work with parents in controlling their children's caloric intake and in emphasizing nutritious foods. They should be the gatekeepers for access to medical and counseling services that can help with the problem of student obesity.

Appendix

Fiction for Children and Youth on Coping with Obesity

For Young Readers

DuBois, William Pene. *Porko von Popbutton*. New York: Harper & Row, 1968. (Gr. 3-5)

Kroll, Steven. *Fat Magic*. Ill. by Tomie de Paola. New York: Holiday House, 1978. (picture book)

Pinkwater, Manus. *Fat Elliot and the Gorilla*. New York: Four Winds, 1974. (Gr. 2-5)

Solot, Mary Lynn. *100 Hamburgers: The Getting Thin Book*. Ill. by Paul Galdone. New York: Lothrop, Lee & Shepard, 1972. (picture book, Gr. 2-4)

Stevens, Carla. *Pig and the Blue Flag*. Ill. by Rainey Bennett. New York: Seabury, 1977. (Gr. 1-2)

For Middle-Grade Readers

Byars, Betsy. *After the Goat Man*. Ill. by Ronald Himler. New York: Viking, 1974. (Gr. 5-8)

Danziger, Paula. *The Cat Ate My Gymsuit*. New York: Delacorte, 1974. (Gr. 6-9)

DeClements, Barbara. *Nothing's Fair in Fifth Grade*. New York: Viking, 1981. (Gr. 4-6)

Greene, Constance C. *A Girl Called Al*. Ill. by Byron Barton. New York: Viking, 1969. (Gr. 5-8)

Holland, Isabelle. *Dinah and the Green Fat Kingdom*. Philadelphia: Lippincott, 1978. (Gr. 5-8)

Kerr, M.E. *Dinky Hocker Shoots Smack!* New York: Harper & Row, 1972. (Gr. 6-9)

Konigsburg, E.L. *Altogether, One at a Time*. Ill. by Gail E. Haley, Mercer Mayer, Gary Parker, and Laurel Schindelman. New York: Atheneum, 1972. (four separate stories. See "Camp Fat." Gr. 4-7)

Orgel, Doris. *Next Door to Xanady*. Ill. by Dale Payson. New York: Harper & Row, 1979. (Gr. 5-7)

Perl, Lila. *Hey, Remember Fat Glenda?* New York: Houghton Mifflin, 1981. (Gr. 6-9)

Smith, Doris Buchanan. *Last Was Lloyd*. New York: Viking, 1981. (Gr. 5-7)

Smith, Robert Kimmel. *Jelly Belly*. Ill. by Bob Jones. New York: Delacorte, 1981. (Gr. 5-8)

Van Leeuwan, Jean. *I Was a 98-Pound Duckling*. New York: Dial, 1972. (Gr. 6-8)

For Older Readers

Brancato, Robin F. *Come Alive at 505*. New York: Alfred A. Knopf, 1980. (Gr. 9-12)

Lipsyte, Robert. *One Fat Summer*. New York: Harper & Row, 1977. (Gr. 7-10)

Sachs, Marilyn. *Class Pictures*. New York: Dutton, 1980. (Gr. 7-10)

Stolz, Mary. *In a Mirror*. New York: Harper & Row, 1975. (Gr. 9-12)

For information on fitness programs for the mentally retarded, contact:

Joseph P. Kennedy, Jr. Foundation
719 13th Street NW
Washington, DC 20005

For information on sound nutrition, contact:

The American Nutritionists Association
P.O. Box 34030
Bethesda, MD 20817

American Dietetic Association
Department 12
208 South LaSalle Street
Suite 1100
Chicago, IL 60604-1003

References

American Alliance for Health, Physical Education, Recreation, and Dance. *Aerobic Fitness for the Moderately Retarded*. Reston, Va., 1980.

Dietz, W.H. "Childhood Obesity." In Richard J. and Judith J. Wurtman, Eds., *Human Obesity. Annals of the New York Academy of Sciences* 499 (1987).

Feldman, W.; McGrath, P.; and O'Shaughnessy, M. "Adolescents' Pursuit of Thinness." *American Journal of Disabled Children* 140 (1986): 140.

Javernick, E. "Johnny's Not Jumping: Can We Help Obese Children?" *Young Children* 43, no. 2 (1988).

Mellin, L.M. "Adolescent Obesity." *Contemporary Nutrition* 12, no. 8 (1987).

Story, M., and Alton, I. "Nutrition Issues and Adolescent Pregnancy." *Contemporary Nutrition* 12, no. 1 (1987).